The Verdant Realm Of Longing And Loss

A synopsis of Soulful thoughts of a young mind!

Shambhavi Sharma

BookLeaf
Publishing

India | USA | UK

Made with ❤ on the BookLeaf Publishing Platform
www.bookleafpub.in
www.bookleafpub.com

Dedication

To everyone-

Those who are lost or have choked on their own words,
Who have decimated their value and are going bitter,

I hope that you heal from it all and find your solace here.

Preface

Emotions are the threads that weave our lives together. This collection of poems explores the intricate dance of human emotions, from the warmth of love to the chill of grief, and from the turmoil of doubt to the reassurance of belief. These poems explore all the in-betweens of contentment and sorrow and of anguish and anger. And above all, nature's composure and myth's enigma serve as the stage on which this melody lingers upon.

Acknowledgements

To my parents, Thank-you for tolerating me and my tantrums throughout this journey and for supporting me through all my highs and lows AND for your precious guidance as well. I'm forever grateful to you both.

I'm also thankful to my best friends for believing in me without a doubt and to all of my friends who somehow managed to be nothing but encouraging. (Though some of you might have overreacted, but that's fine too).

And lastly thanks to all the factors (known and unknown, discreet and obvious) which made this book possible and to everyone who will read this book, Thank-you for choosing this one.

There`s no light in this world that never fades,
Then there must be no darkness which never subsides.

1. Little Author

Fly, little author,
You were born for the sky.
Go, little author,
It's worth the try.

Listen, little author,
It's okay to cry.
Wipe, little author,
Tears take time to dry.

Swim, little author,
The ocean is your hymn.
Make haste, little author,
But don't decide on a whim.

Breathe, little author,
You're far from the brim.
Relax, little author,
No monsters crawl under your skin.

Walk, little author,
Though the path is unknown.
Rest, little author,
You've certainly grown.

Wake up, little author,
You're worthy, you have shown.
Yes, little author,
You did it on your own.

2. Little Author (2)

Soar high, little author,
With no fear of falling too deep.
You don't fear risks, little author,
This courage you must keep.
Stay afloat, little author,
You won't drown in the sea.
Nature is your home, little author,
The child of where you'll always be.
Everything, little author,
Comes to an end.
However, little author,
If it comes, you just need to mend.
Don't give up, little author,
You have destinations to reach.
Live, little author,
Find joy in your existence, I beseech.
Only then, little author,
You'll unearth the peace that you seek.

3. The 7 Sins

Do you know the root of other sins,
Those who lead towards eternal damnation.
The egregious vices,that always win,
Let me introduce you,The 7 sins-

First comes Lucifer, The sin of pride,
If you ever see him ,run and hide.
He is the leader of the fallen,
Adversary to God, is how they call him.

Then comes Leviathan, The sin of envy,
A sea serpent, deceitful as he can be.
He is the harbinger of chaos and resentment,
Beware of him, lest havoc is your intent.

Here comes Amon, The sin of wrath,
You'll be consumed in flames,If you cross his path.
He is engulfed in inferno, has burning eyes,
You'd be wise to decipher that he isn't nice.

And comes Belphegor, The sin of sloth,
Apathy and procrastination fosters his growth.
If you see a figure lethargic and lounging,
You should know your downfall is approaching.

So comes Mammon, The sin of greed,
Don't be deceived when he says he is in need.
He is surrounded by gold and precious jewels,
Beware his toothy snares and the tales he tells.

Now comes Beelzebub, The sin of gluttony,
Devouring you is his first priority.
He is surrounded by decay and overindulgence,
Stay away when you sight upon extravagance.

When you see Asmondeus, The sin of lust,
Stay far away ,Don't give him your trust.
You'll feel like you've seized a prize,
While he leads you to your own demise.

Don't be bewitched by their tempting smiles,
Don't fall prey to their pretense of kin,
For they are the epitome of annihilation.
Let me conclude ,The 7 sins.

4. And Off We Go

To a distant journey, off we go,
With a little of love and abundant malice to sow,
To discard what little sense is left,
And adopt the ways the world will show.

Do you find your peace?
Do you find your cure?
Do you find you pace?
Until it's wholly yours?

Be a flower that in its wake,
Leaves its traces for the world's sake,
That stays till the crack of dawn,
And even after its last breath is drawn.

It's good that it's dark,
Now no one will be able to see the tears that depart from
my eyes,
The tears that I shed for you tonight.

5. Sweet Candy Talks

Sweet candy talks,
Those lovely yesterday's,
Won't last for tomorrow,
Won't last for today,
Won't last forever, for us anyways.

6. Gone

Gone are the days,
Gone are you,
Gone is my mind,
I have lost my que.
Gone are your traces,
Gone is my screw,
Gone is my purpose,
I'm feeling the blues.
Gone are the remnants
Left of you,
Gone is my sight,
I have forsaken my hue.
Gone are your tantrums,
Gone is the clue,
Gone is my night,
I have long been overdue.

7. My Lease On Earth

When my lease on earth is up,
When I cross the river of life,
When I open afterlife's door,
All I'll ever want to glance upon at first,
Is you my love,
Is you my love.

8. If Only

If only R.I.P. meant
Reality Is Preposterous,
If only I meant you,
If only you meant forever,
We would've too.

If only L.I.F.E. didn't mean
Love Is Facing the End,
If only you weren't God lent,
If only our fate wasn't so twisted,
Unfortunately, now I can only lament.

If only G.O.N.E. meant
Good One's Never End,
If only paradise had a pathway,
If only this was all an illusion,
Then, I'd have found the strength to list what I wished to
convey.

But none of this is so,
And none would come true,
I try to be optimistic,
So that I find me a moment I did not rue.

Would you still be here?
Would you've been here with me today?
If all these were real?
Alas! Death is the price love has to pay.

When the sun, stars and moon collide,
Let`s meet again in afterlife.

9. Starlit Sky

Sometimes I think of you and I,
Someday beneath the starlit sky.
Quietly on the ground we'll lie,
Watching the dance of the fireflies.
The tipsy stars will hum and sing,
For the moon ,the night Brings.
We will sing along without a care,
Leaving behind Our worldly affairs.

10. A Special Day

Today is a special day,
Although the past was a bit too full of dismay.
But scars are a necessary ingredient to success,
And hope is one blessing which allows us to progress.
All that I wish is all that I say,
All that I say is all that I pray.
May you get all that you need and achieve all that you
must,
And when you're not sure of yourself, remember in you
we trust.
There were many beautiful and bittersweet moments
that we spent,
There are many more to come and with the old ones
they'll blend.
And as the end draws near, we'll greet each other with
tears,
And thank the years we got, which accommodated our
fears.

11. Would You?

Would you love me the same,
Even after hearing the crackle in my bones?
Even when decades have passed,
And I am no longer young and bold?

Would you love me the same,
Would your love really stay?
Will you not falter when a day comes,
Where I'm added to you as a burden, as a pain?

12. Yes, I Will.

Yes, I will love you all the same,
Even when your bones aren't strong enough.
Even when centuries have passed,
And you've aged and have started to cough.

Yes, I will love you all the same,
The vows I took with you were not just for fame.
I won't ever falter ,never in a millennium,
You were never a burden ,you were my answer to them.

13. A Single Dime

The hours go by like a passing breeze,
And dawn is breaking, so they tease.
I'll hold you tight and close my eyes,
Will keep you right by my side.
Soon you'll be freed from these earthly restraints,
But for now, let me hug you with all I can.
I won't trade this feeling for a single dime,
'cuz I'm well aware that as such, there'll come no other
time.

14. Love at First Sight

He fell for her freckles,
She fell for his smile,
He fell for the unspoken tale in her eyes,
She fell for the curiosity he fostered inside,
Both of 'em were craving each other's company,
In the hour of darkness they crept into each other's core,
The nights felt ever so lively and were ever so bright,
Even the onlookers felt this rendezvous,
Oh! And of course,
it was love at first sight
it was love at first sight.

At nights sometimes I silently weep,
`cuz there are memories I need to keep.

15. Missing You at Midnight

They say you don't realize the value of some things until
they are gone forever,
I know it's true ,Now I do,
I'm so sorry ,I never fully appreciated you.
But now that you're gone, now that you're no more,
I lay at my bed every night, looking at your photo,

And cry and sob with an aching heart who's denying
that you've departed,
What is this cruelty, this utter misery that has befallen
unto me?
I hadn't loved you enough ,I wasn't done ,I had to say a
lot to you, and I wanted you to be,
just keep being my one and only.

My brain might have accepted the fact, but I look for you
every morning I wake,
And then the sudden realization that you're gone will
always be the worst hit I'll take.

I wish I had a few more hours ,no just a few more
minutes, so I could've said sorry,
Sorry for all the nuisance I had been,
Sorry I couldn't hug you, and kiss you for that one last
time, and this has been my deepest regret since.

16. My Turtle Friend

Today I lost my turtle friend ,
He crossed heaven's door as he reached life's end.
I heard a saying that "God knows best",
And that's why I think she took you to her nest.
They say it'll be alright and that it's okay,
And though it may be true, I'm too selfish to keep my
tears at bay.
While you're gone it's a total distress,
I try not to turn myself into a complete mess.
It's hard, it's hard to live on,
Just to wake up everyday to realize that you're gone.
People may say "why cry,it's just a turtle?"
But they love money more than themselves why can't I
love a turtle.
While you and I are now lives apart,
The memories are etched forever in our hearts.
I wake up every morning and endure the pain,
Just in the hopes that we'll be reunited once again.

17. Time Won't Heal

I'm grieving, please give me time,
A season or two won't help me forget my pain or make
me fine.

I'm mourning, please wait calmly,
There are moments which leave me sore and scar me.

There are times I cry like a maniac, and then there are
times I freely smile,
But when I do, I think of him, and all of it seems so
worthwhile.

I seldom get inside my head to switch, replay, and
rewind,
I'm still waiting to be healed of the hurt, that came when
he left me behind.

Time won't heal, I yelled and cried,
Because even Time can't bring back that piece of me
which left with him, when he died.

18. And I Lost You

I have seen your eyes,now they're devoid of hope,
What there once was, is not anymore.
Where you once flinched to my touch,
You lie motionless at life's shore.

You jumped at the sound of my footsteps,
Now you've drowned ,you seem torn.
You had that charisma, which captivated me,
Now it's faded, and you're mourned.

All these cherished moments, Dawning upon my soul,
Wish that I thanked you a little bit more.
And I lost you, It's eating away at me,
No one, but you can heal my wounded core.

Your departure has dampened the flickering hope,
Bits and pieces of me are lost, and you're not here to
make me whole.
How I regret not mentioning it often-
Thank-you, for lighting up my world.

Your words have turned into daggers,
Which now penetrate my very existence.

19. Echoes Of Anguish: A Cycle

I am incased in this interminable cycle of pain,
With nothing to lose and nothing to gain,
While I sit in numbness I grasp the tale,
All of my affection, my efforts, my empathy, my love,
every wee bit of them is now in vain.

20. Echoes Of Anguish: Pieces

The laughter that broke to a cry,
The smile that turned to tears,
The voice that succumbed to silence,
And the gaze that burned with fears.

It was enough to make me shudder,
Enough to pierce through my Heart,
To Tear it into pieces,
And gradually Rip it apart.

The pieces shattered on the ground,
Were Crushed into millions with emotions fueled,
And Vanished forth myself,
How was it ok and still not cruel?

21. Want It To End

Something suddenly strikes me at midnight,
And that is where my perfect life torments,
I go perfectly silent ,Numb, turn and toss, groan in pain,
And that is where I want it to end.

I feel so desolated ,I can't even render,
And there is but ,little left to my forbearance,
So I wish my days were numbered,
And that's where I want it to end.

22. Not Your Pastime Toy

So, if you desire, she is vulnerable,

And when you wish, she is invincible?

Well, you failed, my friend,

She is the tune that calms the soul of the night when you
have contaminated it with your wickedness,

She is the gust of wind that blows as a breeze to soothe
the mind of the aggrieved after you've indulged in
deviousness.

She is that holy water that is sprinkled wherever you go
to mask your corruptness.

She is the very incantation of the fallen,

A woman woven by the threads of destiny,

She is the verse sang by the angels choir,

A flower that in its wake leaves its traces forever even
after wilting,

She is beauty incarnate herself,

She is all but your favorite pastime toy, my darling.

Yet, you think her fragile, your grasp a mere shadow,

Blind to the fire that dances beneath her skin,

Her laughter, a storm that shatters your hollow bravado,

Her silence, a sword that cuts through the din.

So tread carefully on this sacred ground,

For beneath the surface of her grace lies a power
profound.

She is all but your favorite pastime toy.

23. The Audacity

And lo ,it's here,
Once again, it's so near.
I gotta admit, the audacity is sheer,
Am I capable of overcoming this fear?

I did, I paid,
I swear, I said.
Then why are they afraid,
Of the monster they have made.

In days so gloomy and so dull, where I`m hiding beneath
a facade,
I find myself constantly slipping into your sweetest
embrace.

24. An Actor

You look at me, as if I'm an icon, brave and bold,
With a fiery passion in my eyes and demeanour ice cold,
You think that I'm all-knowing, that I've it all figured out,
That my life is a smooth sailing boat, upon which I'm on
and about.

But if you look close enough, if you try to take a sneak
peak,
You'll see the fear in my eyes, a fright very peculiar, an
anxiety very keen,
And you'll know that I'm an actor and which I've been,
An actor performing on the stage of life who's learning
from experience.

25. WIND

The rustling of wind,
The misty blanket unveils the moon,
Gelid tipsy bliss.

26. The Echoes Of The Wild

The day passed just right,
Mostly rainy but still bright.
The sun shimmered amidst the silken threads,
With subtle wind, on emerald beds.

The petrichor smell of soil,
Revived the vitality muffled in turmoil.
The greyish sky and muddy road,
Embroider wonder, lightening the mood.

Yet the most awaited part that I crave,
Is the night, I must say.
The chirping cricket and hooting owl,
Still, what I covet to hear, is the lone wolf's howl.

The beguiling smirk of the crescent moon,
Tore through the twilight's tune.
I leisurely indulge in the moonlit grace,
Finding tranquillity in nature's embrace.

27. Poetry

I may not love a single molecule of me,
But I so love all my pieces of poetry ,
And the poems I write are who I am,
Thus, I love myself, too dearly.